IN AN ERA OF PILLAGE

ANON EDITION

2022
Flagstaff   Stockton

SOTÈRE TORREGIAN

IN AN ERA OF PILLAGE

Edited and designed by Richard Waara
Front and back covers by Sotère Torregian
Marie Wilson's *Eagle Spirit* by permission of the Valaoritis family

ISBN 978-1-4116-8874-2

To the loving memory of my former wife
Kathleen Brummal (1945-2021)

Le labyrinthe qui remonte la valleuse à toute allure et brûle toutes les mosquées »

XXIX — S.J.

Preface, or My Last Will and Testament?

There are many voices as I write. I find myself a stranger amongst them. In a recent *Star Trek* rerun Captain Jean Luc Picard of the Starship Enterprise finds himself transported in time back to the year 1941. I found myself recognizing those streets—the cityscape, the automobiles, the women's clothes, the bustle of the city when I was born in my first natal birth. My second birth, which occurred at age 17, was by way of French Surrealism. Long before then poems had issued from me but they could find no real habitation, yet they did so when I was embraced, or should say was enveloped, by SURREALISM and by the words of the Manifestos of André Breton and his fellow friends and poets, Paul Éluard, Robert Desnos, as well as Max Jacob's *Le Cornet à dés,* Guillaume Apollinaire's inaugural surrealist drama *Les Mamelles de Tirésias,* and eventually the Négritude Movement of Léopold Sédar Senghor and Aimé Césaire, which summoned my ancestors' *métis Africanité* in my blood. That became intermingled with my Mediterranean origins, thereafter displaced by immigration to Newark, New Jersey, as my grandparents emigrated to America from the island of Sicily. As I grew up I have likened it to what I imagine it is like growing up in the xenophobic atmosphere of Chinatown in San Francisco, with its own customs, feasts and foreign speech, and with no real sense of the outside world of White America. I then felt as I do now as ever an immigrant, displaced, without a homeland.

I came to despise my surroundings—the Anglo world whereupon I had involuntarily been deposited and displaced. In school I had been forced to recite the Pledge of Allegiance and to sing the discordant notes of "The Star-Spangled Banner," the words for which I could never understand and which I mispronounced, unbeknownst to those kids, singing away, around me. As a student I was a daydreamer, who transported himself, as in Keats' poem "Sleep and Poetry," to another world outside the windows of the schoolroom, which I eventually discovered to be SURREALITY.

There, beyond any ethnicity, or internecine of countries, of "God, King, and Country" mouthed by political bigots, I, having graduated from prison (school), at the age of 19, to the utter disappointment of my relatives (but with the empathy of my mother), dared to declare myself a poet as my "profession," emerging out of obscurity to give my public debut, the first reading of my poems, in 1963—the pivotal year (age 22)—at the Café Le Metro coffeehouse, New York City, amidst the warmth and friendship of such poet pals as Ted Berrigan, Joe Ceravolo, Ted Joans and John Ashbery into the intervening years of the late Sixties.

Thence, a flurry of books and unpublished manuscripts followed, which to my amazement, I authored by my own hand. How could that be, I asked? But it is. I still ask it to this day.

Still, I consider myself, as Paul Valéry declared of himself *"un amateur de poesie."* This is to be understood not as in the English meanings as an amateur but in the French as *a lover of poetry.*

Hence, many voices have merged or emerged in these, what I like to call, *automatiques,* with the earliest to the latest gathered here. Perhaps, as days go by, they may constitute my Last Will and Testament to my audience of readers.

And I will travel as a stranger amongt these many voices of mine, which are gathered here under a name of one almost unbeknownst to me—SOTÈRE TORREGIAN, who remains on the planet without visa.

I am I, now 500 years old.
My future bride will find me mummified in this book.

S.T.

...le saccage du grand coeur des saisons
—Aimé Césaire, *Moi, laminaire, 1982*

("...the ransacking of the great heart of the seasons")

THE IMAGE OF YOUTH

"Beginnings" (1955-1957)

The image of youth, Chatterton lying lifeless on his couch
and I, yet again, lying on my mother's red sofa
whiling away the afternoon of a humdrum day

I count the hours
although at age 17 I already feel a 100
waiting for some new discovery
enclosed in this family home of Fairmount

I am surrounded by Bulls of Bashan
crucified by school-rules phantasms—
conformity's curse of the Fifties
with the prospect of bullies again the next day

My father's Mexican masks acquired by theft in his travels
and the statue of a horse whose gallop is frozen in time
look down at me from the mantelpiece

Even as my dreams of the Polish Princess
enemy beloved of the young Cossack Taras Bulba
dissipate into nothingness

Yet even as I, a dispossessed refugee, am utterly alone here
I dream of conquests and the unattainable
over bullies and their exalters, over standards of relatives
and the judgments of naysayers which befall me

This darksome image of myself in the mirror
which constantly accuses me of failure and defeat...
yet I refuse, a recusant

In the Silence that envelopes me

1

However distant I begin to heed within
the "still small voices" of the soul
It is poetry which is its clarion that leads me
to my own recognition of my true self
that which remains ever unknown to others

The I that ultimately is—
The Master of Life that I am meant to be
even as it may be worlds away

Newark, N.J.
(reconstructed from fragments
of a poem in a journal, 1957)

KLEPHTIC-SOULED

for Geneviéve Del Sordi

I am of the Klephts
to steal her away from her lover
In the December approach of strangers
I "played it by ear"

Spasms of flesh and bone

Inasmuch an impuissant Perseus
to free her from him who possessed her
now disturbed from sleep
(And afterward I found myself
in the attempt
held captive there)

As she spoke "I cannot..."
in whispers
as I interposed
into her dream

And watched *bouleversant**
from the promontory
klephtic-souled
the breaking point of
an almost-attained heaven
    fast-receding

I remained struck
upon the rungs of time

Newark, N.J.
Summer, 1961

**bouleversant, Fr.,* upsetting
Note: The Klephts were Greek Independence fighters, especially ones who fought
the Turks in the 15th century or during the war of independence (1821-1828).

3

THE #54 BUS

O great moth jowls dripping in blood
with the nostalgia of a thousand centuries
with your soot lashing in my eye

Window zoo animal of autumn
skunk of summer
snowman of winter
Don Juan of nude mannequins!

Spinster in the ticket-box pouring out her false eyelashes

Bells clanging for the cataloguer

The drachmas of my eyes speed the 25 mph limit

Back at my vacant lot on 18th Street
Cerberus guards the door to where
I come home every night

1965

4

FAST-FALLING TREE BUDS, SPRING, 1966

for Calvin Forbes
(after reading in the Sunday paper "Remember The Dead of Gettysburg")

Fast-falling tree buds
my entrance into fratricide
like green snow
the Dead of Gettysburg

We are not in Pennsylvania
Thunder at the door
Boys with blowtorches working
over the latest stolen car

Sunday papers, Sunday funnies

You have grown
My hands dirty
a song-like oboe serves as a bridge
predisposed to gyre-render
the safety-bolt of the extreme day

Comported through the long utility
of time static and infinitesimal
Icarian gate
booming with squashed roots

My wife my love
you sleep in the morning bed I made for you
here carrying the church outside on my shoulder

Unhorsing
Spring worlds
which Isaac gave back to Abraham

O music and ears
of 18 year olds on street walls!

Newark, N.J.
1966

DEATH OF ANDRÉ BRETON (Sept. 29th 1966)

for Philip Lamantia (in San Francisco)

Leave me desolate here
on this street where I bear myself
forever walking this morning
not knowing wheresoever I am going

A Yakut with arctic ear-laps on
for no apparent reason
I rush onto ramparts where there is no foe to confront

No one hears me as my agonized cry goes skyward

I have eaten the meal of forgetfulness
I do not know whether it is day or night
Whether I am a free man or a slave
but that I am molten

Suddenly the whole panorama in front of me at 7PM
turns into a browned photo postcard
The music of the spheres plays a contrapuntal chorus of "Burn
all water!" and "Drown all fire!" as André ascends--

> O Goufre!* Goufre! Goufre!
>
> O Goufre! Goufre! Goufre!

Mon frère ! Maître Inivisble ! You continue to walk in my shadow.
Your empire realizes the infinite enactment of Poetry

O monumental expanse! The overhanging breasts of Nût!
Upholder of the sky where you are!

Newark, N.J.
30th September, 1966

*Goufre, Fr., Chasm

6

THE MERIDIAN ENCAPSULATES

The meridian encapsulates my transatlantic hope
I'm captured by a crane uplifting across your domain
    by the seat of my pants
Wings are burning held for a moment by a cloud
Gives you time to sleep and be a bearer of percolators
    to topple Stonehenge   The arc of a window
dances about being difficult

        No ends to the remains
of a child's nightgown holding the boat of hours
In a lantern trance O boat of hours!
Hush! A child passing through a wave of hands at prayer

"Grace" in the language of pomegranates
bleeding inside a tortured palm   I know
what's on your mind!
Thorns! With roses falling

It's time to climb inside my cantatrice
before the club-footed lion beaches us
Forgetful of my envelope with nail-clippings as is my wanton
    character of inertia   I sweat lighthouse dreams

                Kathleen Brummal-Torregian
                & Sotère Torregian,
                   New York, 1966

Note: This collaborative "automatique" poem was written just before my then-wife, Kathleen, and I prepared to leave New York for the West Coast (San Jose, California) to take up residence there in January, 1967. --S.T.

THE BLACK SPRING BECOMES ANONYMOUS

The wind is blowing in the scent of formaldehyde
for the barefoot and the blind
I approach my shadow like a two-gun gunslinger
of the Old West
You get the publicity and your father gets grey hairs
Out of my breath comes the smell of formaldehyde*
        on the Rose of Sharon
and the Rose of Sharon dies

1971

*Alludes to when, after being hunted down in Bolivia by an agent for the CIA, captured, then summarily executed, Che Guevara's two hands were amputated and placed in formaldehyde to preserve his fingerprints.

TO A YOUNG WOMAN STOCKBROKER AT CHARLES SCHWAB & CO.

for Ms. Judy Carlson

Sous une apparance de beauté ou le raison contre tout apparance aussi
("Under the appearance of beauty or the reasons also against all appearance")
—André Breton, *Claire de terre*

The fountains play leapfrog with each other
on the path ahead of me

A herd of eohippi hidden in the eaves

Their impromptu fanfare sounds for me
to introduce myself
once inside your office door

I stand there   finding words   at last
I happen to mention Pushkin whom you say you don't know
as one of my predecessors   descendant also of
one of Africa's peers

That has lead me here today to evoke
lines in praise of Woman's beauty as well as her wiles

You laugh as I confess to you that I have kept
as a souvenir one share of Frederick's of Hollywood stock
which yields zero dividends for me

Yet my only real reason to wander in here today
is to present you with this singular red leaf
(which, as I speak, I realize is a fool's errand
that will wither in time)

Your lithe Asian associate broker on a smoke break
is seated on the bench outside
beige stockings matching hauteur-couture shoes—

I recall a young Sandinista Militia-woman standing guard in
    Managua
and the Spanish word for Beauty... *Belleza*

The news reports "racism on the rise on college campuses"

In the while a grove of orange-blossomed trees
lift up their song
as choristers to the breeze

Sunnyvale, Calif.
1988

Note: This is a variant version of the poem that appeared prior in *On the Planet Without Visa* (2012).

AT THE NEW YEAR

for Mary Ann Caws

> *la nuit qui décalque mes images*
> ("the night which traces my images")
> —André Breton, *Poèmes*

Isn't it wonderful?   You are three hours ahead
of us in the New Year here on the West Coast
and we know less about poetry than ever

My name comes pouring like an endless sea out of a bottle
across *Tarnation!*★ to be received by you
where you stand clad in the guise of the Indian Corn Maiden
                    (which appears on the corn starch box)

You discern the song the sirens sang to Odysseus
I return with your moccasins secured in my teeth
This isn't the legend of Sleepy Hollow
We've secured the skull of Peking Man to play catch with

It is pertinent enough to declare
a skull's hunger for Cocoa Krispies

"Life" can be "summed up" in that one moment
"Man" exists
to prove him/her/self as clumsy as it may sound
not an umbrella-stand

Which enables us
on our parts to be better stokers of the fire

1st—2nd January, 1997

★*Tarnation!* c.f., Li'l Abner comic strip, *circa* 1934-1977.

11

MADAME LE SAUVAGE

qui incendiaiment ma soif
("which ignited my thirst")
—L.S. Senghor, *Nocturnes*

In what wood do you hide, Mme. Le Sauvage?
Is it the Bois de Boulogne
or St. John's Wood?

I can't find your can of soda you sipped from
and then turned demurring into lioness or bird
I can't find the taste of your mouth in mine

Although I know it has become mixed in my wine

And as I walk about on my errands
I trace the pale of your autumnal plumage
(reminiscently given by the spellbound Inca
to the seemingly dissembling Pizarro)
I can't find the shudder of your touch next to my skin

In what giant sea-conch then do you go to retire
and to seductively recline there on a divan
like Monte Cristo's Haydee in the shimmer
of her odalisque gaze?

I can't find the moment
in which you move
from here to "there"

2001

IN AN ERA OF PILLAGE

The dust of Balzac settles on everything
Wipe it away and in a few days the dust returns
and settles again   On treasures, or the spoils of
war, on bridal-photos...on all that I would hold sacred

As long as there is gravity, as long as there are
sunbeams to transport it (but the dust settles as
well by night)...I keep my typewriter covered
but should I forget and leave it exposed, the dust
settles there and even clogs the keys...

So, Balzac travels beyond himself

And so we travel...There is no hadj but to the
hadj within ourselves   As the great Athenian sage
Socrates said "No matter where we travel we take
ourselves with us and return to ourselves"

(*Memento homo quia   pulvis es...**)

But dust does not cover the invisible where the laws of
gravity do not operate

Thus the *hadj*

Viens, lui répondit sou père en le prenant
par la main et l'amenant dans la grande salle**

2002

---

* *"Remember man that you are dust" (Lat.)*
** *"Come on, his father answered, taking him by the*
hand and bringing him into the great room" (Fr.)

13

ON HIROSHIMA REMEMBRANCE DAY

for Paula Sheil

It's too late now I think   I've been awake
now these many hours   "Best time
            for contemplative works
of the soul or mind"   is 4AM
                        according to Ibn al-Arabi
....

Yet that human codicil

displayed at Hiroshima's Peace Park
its clock hand
            barely stopped at 8AM...

                  portends "Carpe Diem"

On the other hand, closer to home
there's always the opportunity
for us to be
            tourists
visiting the site of the slaves' quarters at Mt. Vernon

            Soon I'll hear the rush of the shower
of my pretty neighbor next door
while she readies herself for her
workday   I remain here
as مسافر musafir   journeying
in my mind that seems to go nowhere

Before the mirror I hear myself tell myself:
"Your ribs are showing!"

                        6th August, 2003

14

YOUR LETTER'S ENVELOPE MARKS THE PAGES OF A BOOK

for Christa Marle O'Neal

A child in faraway Tennessee
reads the word "Didymus"
from off the envelope's return address

What light
from yon window breaks East

My left ear still itches

It is always instructional
to know what day of the week it is

But all this week by my cuneiform calendar
it seemed like
it was always the same day

There is no African cure for
the fear of death but the joy of the palm-wine drinkard

Yet never has labour been so mobilized
despite my faulty French translation

$$Hélas\star$$
as your singular rose still keeps
its saffron colour illumining the night
as you walk into the room

December, 2004

Hélas, Fr., Alas

FOR LARA LOGAN

Or je hantais la ville de vos songes
("Now I haunted the city of your dreams")
—St.-John Perse, *Anabasis*

In you the demarcations of East and West
meet and wring their hands
    I myself pat my Teddy on the head (who is as good a sentry
on my bed   brave as those mechanical marchers
in the Changing of the Guard
at Lenin's tomb in Moscow

I have spoken
to the moon   that tells me in response
of its vacation
these last two years   in your bodice
                       Mon chére aventuriére !*

which leaves me in effect
speechless as a ziggurat

                I regain only
to confess
I have never learned to tell military time
but in this hour (which gives birth like an oyster)
I present
to you the Moor of Venice's handkerchief

        O non troppo assai!**

As on it a tear appears in the form
of a minute chandelier

                      31st December, 2004

**Mon chére aventuriére ! Fr., My dear adventurer!*
***O non troppo assai! It., Or not so much!*

16

LOST IN TRANSLATION AGAIN

for Anya Wozniak-Brayman

It remains then   after all
a matter of translation
I am lost in translation

The bowwow language of yelping dogs
that Man first heard   then mimicked
climbing down from the trees

And then   how *do* we
translate "Man" whom has five-billion Woman-souls in "him"

How is Love, that Love the immortal
Florentine described as "*L'Amor
che move il sole el'altre stelle*"* in his *Paradiso*?

That Love which moves the sun
and the *other* stars to be translated
kiss to pubis   to the everyday of our lives?

Last night I laid barren
and this morning my pen bears
fruit   And now that bloom
comes to you as it came to me
by a beautiful woman's words over thousands of miles

Africa remains untranslated   The bones and reliquaries
of saints have been translated

2004

*"*L'Amor che move il sole el'altre stelle*," It.*, Love that moves the sun and other stars.

17

FOR SOPHIE (IN PARIS) AT THE APPROACH OF FALL

*Mais chante sur mon absence tes yeux de brise alizés,
et l'Absente soit présence* ("But let your eyes of trade-
wind breeze sing upon my absence, and may the Absent
Woman return") —L.S. Senghor, *Élégie des alizés*

My fingers in idleness make the sound of drumming
a horse's hooves in a gallop
then halting (perhaps rearing itself
at an inn   its phantom horse's head
become a road-sign)
all re-enacted on the hard
cover of a book
just picked up this morning
as I loll waiting to rise
from my bed
                Far away I hear
the TV announcer's prattle
In a moment I note   the hands of
the clock have already moved   into another hemisphere

Here I long for the fragrance of your hair
perhaps with its scent of spikenard with which maidens
were anointed before entering the labyrinth of the Minotaur

12th September, 2005

ON AIMÉ CÉSAIRE'S AND MY BIRTHDAY

*Le synthèse admet un coefficient supérieur, un surcroit de
conscience de la conscience* ("The synthesis admits a higher
coefficient, an increase in consciousness of consciousness")
—Gerard Legrand, *S'appuyant sur Hegel*

I think "What shall I *do* today, *ah*?" (There's that "Ah-ha"
moment of Oprah)—At least, give something away. I won't have
to unplug the toilet today. I can walk around, purchase calamari
maybe at the market (but ultimately have to change my mind as
my daughter objects, being a "Vegan"). Buy myself a bran muffin
instead. Perhaps *reinvent* The City of Chicago? *Hmm.* Write Dénis
Roche again although he hasn't answered my last 5 letters. Be
jubilant that Paris Hilton will be released from prison today.
OPEN THE PRISONS, DISBAND THE ARMY! *Aimé ami,* I
hope someone's provided you with an amaranthine pipe and
winged slippers today. In my hands I hold a limited edition of
Balzac (*La Comédie humaine*). Its gold leaf shines like a mirror
onto the "external world." Man-and-Womankind are still
voyageurs and I the *voyeur.* "The synthesis admits of a higher
coefficient" you say, old friend? My lovely muse hasn't forgotten.
She's left a gift on my doorstep *hush, hush* as she hurried off to
work this morning.

25th June, 2007

FOR THE PAINTER TARUN BEDI, ROME, ITALY

A child has dropped a gold star on the path

As I steal out the door
to post some last minute letters
                                        at dusk
my neighbors won't notice my shoes coming apart

The Tigris and Euphrates still flow on
                            (tinged with blood)

O homindae!   Auguri!   Ardi!
My shadow now makes its hajj
to Freud's consultation room in Vienna   its walls
covered with oriental carpets   a stream one must wade
surrounds the patient's couch

"A plume of words" (Anne Waldman)

O meadows and thickets   of an embrace remembered
disappeared at the bus-shelter   Upon my return
I wander from one end of my room to the other
in the *coquille** of a beggar rather than a shepherd

The child's gold star glimmers still on the wet
pavement trodden by passersby

October, 2009

*coquille, Fr., shell

20

AGAIN THE PRICE OF GOLD: NEW YEAR'S EVE

for Tarun Bedi

Always the same question: Where do we go from here when
"Here is always 'fickle'"(says my Brother Tarun Bedi, speaking
on the phone from Rome). At this moment I could fall asleep
even though there's a giant fireworks display going on in Sydney.
Amongst these one must count the implications of Freud's
conceptions of the self at the moment Vanna (White) shows
America on TV how to eat a banana. *Klaxons* (taxicab horns)
are no longer made in Paris. And as for me, Amy Robach, I can
no longer sip, *mon chèrie,* champagne from your slipper.
Like Dagwood I'm in the kitchen in quest of a midnight snack.
My preference is to dine on black-eyed peas rather than to hear
them sing. Here are fragments of confetti and ticker-tape falling
from Times Square, NYC, like volcanic ash falling as red snow
on Pompeii. Step into the world of 21st Century Dentistry: the
appetite of the beast eating one woman's sex after another to
satisfy its male prowess, a white man's face singing in the same
intonation and voice a black man's music, and the world of
"corporate intelligence." The last two words are not coeval. How
do you "parse" that information to maximize the shareholders?
You never embarked with the many-decked ships for Troy the
body-language we are conscious of, or not.

Equitable　　just fair　　*Fantôme*　　*plusiers*

*"That re-minting of the brain when all its partition walls seem to give
way."*

2009

21

A WOMAN'S SILVER SLIPPER FOUND ON THE GROUND FROM THE NIGHT BEFORE

for Lola Koundakjian

Et les formes qui s'attardent
("And the shapes that linger")
—Aimé Césaire, *Noria*

A woman's silver slipper found on the ground this morning
as I emerge from my door (no doubt left from the carouse
of the night before) transports me between time and space
onto the path of my own lost footsteps
"here" contrary to Heraclitus'
"you cannot step twice into the same river"
and one cannot be in two places at once   I find my way
    between
bulls and bear ready to scrimmage
at the opening bell of the New York Stock Exchange

The mystery of language itself from the first migrations
    out of Africa
I don't know my direction in this moment
Giuseppi Verdi's *Atilla* is being played on the stage
as Atilla struts over the smouldering ruins of Aquileia
The shape of a woman's lithe leg and foot
The sable venus ready to step into the slipper there
only to disappear again in my grasp

My doppelgänger waits with the restless queue of poets
waiting to read at Café Le Metro on Second Avenue
And above flying near Cloud Nine is the bed I slept in
    with the young Romanian princess
Overhead there's a flock of wild geese winging and honking
in the morning haze

March, 2010

22

FOR THE BIRTHDAY OF NELSON MANDELA

I'm here seated in the cockpit   of my desk
at my typewriter   ready for take-off
                              Nelson Mandela
92 years young   this day   We don't have to free him
any longer   So there's no need to sing that song
There have been so many false-starts and yet so many
true ones
              My own life began and ended so many times
since that little makeshift garden outside the prison cell
on Robben Island after Sharpeville and the blood spilt there
sprang up as a nation's Pegasus of martyrs and of *l'Afrique*
I still hear your appeal   Serumaga
to the audience gathered at Stanford's Dinkelspiel Auditorium

Those who may think my writing poems is inconsequential
don't see how invisibly they perform
a pomp and circumstance march that ceremonially joins
the red flag with the tricolour

Allons! In the poet's wine goblet it's neither half-full
nor half-empty   I hold the beginnings of new worlds that which
draws men and women together as bargello knitwork   to be
raised on high each time the name of Mandela is sung

NELSON MANDELA!
WE DON'T HAVE TO FREE YOU ANY LONGER!
IT IS YOU WHO NEEDS TO FREE US!

                              17th July, 2010

OCCUPY LONDON!

for Kai Wargalla

So it happens in the course of human events
I'm well this morning   Thank you   but a couple
of millions of others (I'm sorry to say) aren't quite
I'm happy to be breathing
and to see Spitfire remnants in a V formation in the sky
as they fly over London to celebrate the Queen's Diamond
Jubilee   Bless you the survivors of the war against fascism
Big Ben and St. Paul's fiery blitz are effigies of Pathé news
which still remain as a part of my childhood memory

I don't plan to take any trip soon on a cruise ship
where black children wait with open palms for coins tossed
    by tourists
I don't take refuge in the Buddha
I take refuge in the Globe Theatre
where Lady Macbeth's hands stained with blood are those
of the bankers and their cohorts' foreclosures
the usurers and Tories who applaud
the puppet-show of the Status Quo

There am I in your shadow

That of Tom Joad and of Patrice Lumumba and with Ché
    amongst you
who cry out for *Liberté, égalitié, fraternité*
Words of Man-and-Womankind that inform me
I am no more a "terrorist" than Henry Purcell

                                        October, 2011

24

OCCUPY WALL STREET!

for Ania Aizman

*Et tu tâcheras de saisir le moment le grand
feudataire parcourra* ("And you shall try to seize
the moment the grand feudal lord travels")
—Aimé Césaire, *Les Armes miraculeuses*

As the priest cleanses his chalice   so do I this morning
cleanse my cat's dish first thing
From my father I learned to print the alphabet   My Dad
who was the phantom "Cuban boxer"
from whom I never learned to box and fend off bullies
but everywhere today towns and cities are in upheaval—
HOORAY!

It's $2.16 for the Sunday paper
as usual I give away the store sales' inserts
to Rose   the grocery clerk
I keep only the "funnies" (that's what we use to call them)
the comic-strips "Garfield" and "Sally Forth"
not to forget "Charlie Brown & Co."   I've followed
Prince Valiant's adventures since I was a little boy
and here (can you believe it?) we've reached line 30 already
As the Occupiers gather on Wall Street to demonstrate
Paris must be blowing its nose right now   they're warming up

the Space Station in Kazakhstan gurgles

doesn't take away the ache in my back
only the spell of beauty of the woman I love can
and that only momentarily as she's *l'absente*
But on the other hand it's a joy to see the People rise up
again to sing "AVANTE POPOLO!"*

30th October, 2011

★"*Avante Popolo,*" *It.,* "Go Forward, People!" Anthem of the Italian Communist
Party. We used to sing it during Peace marches in the 1960's. —S.T.

VANNA'S IRIDESCENT YELLOW DRESS

for Vanna White

Tu es... la porte radieuse de grace
("You are...the radiant gate of grace")
—L.S. Senghor, ***Chants d'ombre***

Vanna's iridescent yellow dress
this evening
its yellow ochre invades my silence

I greet it in but a moment's viewing
as a man returning
from journeying the Gobi as a solitary

And as a solitary
I remain holding my pen in hand
as if it were a sorcerer's wand
and with a wave her dress
evermore iridescent
leaves its colour to pervade my world
as she herself appears and disappears

In the same manner as Monet
held his brush at Giverny
to capture and transpose the lily pads
there in the pond onto a canvas

And as sleep comes to herald its entry
the room is lit with gamboge and ochre

As I lie here pondering what it was
Archimedes was drawing in the sand
in his last moments before all went dark

Here my sultanate is established
myself become its chambered nautilus

As I speak as interloper
I see the effluvia of my voice
is of a xanthic hue

The water I pour from the decanter
streams the yellow ochre of her dress

The colour of the room
has changed to an iridescent yellow

And you
who have come upon this testimony
observe the air about you now transposed
to the same yellow of a vibrant flower

4th April, 2013

DANS DE ROUTE SANS BUT

for Nanos Valaoritis

On my bed is the sail of Odysseus   I smell
the brine of the Aegean as I wake   I admit I am
very bad at playing checkers or games in general
It's always been that way   I don't expect it to change
I have difficulty in recalling the names of the planets
and/or their respective symbols, e.g., the ♄ for Saturn

An opportunity to listen in the Silence...

Of islands I think of *Zakynthos*   and of the isle
of Gorée off Senegal where slaves were imprisoned awaiting
their journey of "the Atlantic Passage" to the New World

A single blonde hair on my arm—the rest of my hairs
bespeak my *métissage*★ something she could never quite
    comprehend

—As to the word "home" that evokes my *dépaysment* its nearest
equivalent perhaps being music (which Corelli would
recognize as opposed to the denizens of my own era)

Amongst other things which I "surprise" myself with
it is the continuity
of "Love...that waits in the shadow of every word"★★

April, 2013

Note: *Dans de route sans but, Fr.,* On a goalless road
★ *métissage, F.,* that of African (Cyrenaican) as was attributed to Aesop
★★ Plato, *The Symposium,* "Diôtima's Speech"—

« Δαίμων μέγας... καὶ γὰρ πᾶν τὸ
δαιμόνιον μεταξύ ἐστι θεοῦ τε καὶ θνατοῦ »

MORNING SONG FOR GRETCHEN LOUDIN

*for Ms. Gretchen Loudin, Librarian Extraordinaire, San Joaquin Central
Library, Stockton, California, with eternal gratitude for her services throughout
the years!*

> *J'efface mon image, je souffle ses halos*
> ("I erase my image, blow out its halos")
> —Paul Éluard, *Le Révolution Surréaliste,*
> *No.9-10*

Desperate and insane acts characterize to perpetuate
this society that continues to unravel   As for me
I'm ready
to write at a moment's notice, preferring
the high-jinx solfeggios of Ernie Kovacs' gorilla trio
performing a descant

I'm determined despite impediments
to go out today but not otherwise
than appearing in my *sous-vêtements,* i.e.
clad only in my underwear

There's no reason for me as in Downton Abbey to care
no servant needed to hold my clothes and/or dress me
I depend solely on myself and on the forces of gravity
to assist me   I haven't as yet trained my cat
to be my *valet de chambre*

On the news today there's "All the cash that's looking for
a home"   Well, I'm here and I'm eminently available
Mesdames et Messieurs, I'm ready to be the host for the same!
I can be found in my cave surrounded by boxes in the midst
of piled-high newspapers, books and poetry which fills
the entire space of the room

It's not tomorrow—it's already today!

14th May, 2013

FOR JULIANNA GOLDMAN

Je t'ai boire / l'eau pur du miroir
Ou je m' étais perdu
("I drank you / pure water from the mirror
  Where I was lost")
—Paul Éluard, *Le Château des pavres*

Your hair intones an ever resplendent autumn there
the while in my dark in which I travel
                              French the language
     of my vehicle of oracles
the escutcheon on the package of Old Gold cigarettes
smoke now extinct flurries in the air

Africa
and China   are envious
of your televised conversation and deliberation

You the secreted summer worshipper
          enclosed in a synagogue of wheat
You the dancer in black tights
performing in William Grant Still's ballet
The Prince and the Mermaid

A Royal Arrow (vintage 1935) typewriter sings
your name alone on the blank page
crossed-out superfluous lines
and corrected mistakes
the secrets of Picasso's paintings

The summit achieved   without the mountain
Your dissonant Eros hitherto inaccessible
becomes disclosed to me in the jewel
inside the lotus of sleep

24th September, 2013

Note: Julianna Goldman is a CBS News Washington, D.C.-based correspondent.

THE MYSTERY RESOLVED

for Will Alexander

> *à mi-chemin entre ce qui se fane et ce qui asigne*
> *("halfway between what fades and what sucks")*
> —René Crevel, *Le Grande manniquin*
> *cherche et trouve sa peau*

Yet again another mystery apart
from those giant Moai heads that guard
the shores of Easter Island
                    The enigma of writing itself
from Meroë* remains in the tumult that surrounds Africa
The mystery of gravity remains as my pen
falls to the ground relaxed from my grasp
as I tend to the pot on the stove before it boils over

Does someone step out of the blue to propose
a new monetary policy? You don't have to be
from Brooklyn to know it can ultimately be solved
by distributing the wealth to all the people
Just as I don't expect Guillaume Apollinaire
at any moment to walk through the door as I sit here

Neither will Chicago be of any help
to resolve this mystery which lies within your domain
You the woman I have not known
As my hand passes invisibly to stroke
the corona of your Angevine hair

10th October, 2013

---

*Meroë: ancient African Cushitic kingdom, 800 BCE-350 CE, dubbed "the Athens of Africa." The written language of Meroë has not yet been adequately deciphered by scholars.

31

A WORKER'S GLOVE FALLEN IN THE STREET

for Richard Waara

As I wait to cross the street
it lies there before me
crumpled like a wounded animal
I ache in my limbs   The world
still hates
the wayward domain of the poet

       My own traces
can't be found anywhere
My head a Victrola horn screeches dissonant music
as I wait for the traffic light to change
No crumbs in my pockets to feed the birds foraging in the street

At this point where I stand
fools surround me
Skateboarders incessantly yelping wildly on cellphones
Numquam Kingdom that its Michelob Ultra truck goes by

No one's seen or been excited by
the act of my placing a book into my pouch
Books in these times become derelicts as we live
in a nation of poltroons and cyborg-mercenaries!

Overhead there's a vision of Edward Snowden's nose
with white wings making its way aloft in the clouds
                     —*Arrivederci!*
Anaximander, you are still deceived
The chicken or the egg the road has obliterated
A UPS delivery man nearby pauses for a moment
as I overhear the call on his cellphone
"Hi Mom!" reverberates throughout the ionosphere

                        25th October, 2013

FRANTZ FANON

for Will Alexander

O muted
voice   1956   *Presence Africaine*
You will speak   the Sorbonne
for me   As I sew my pants
here you sewed the hole in my life my existence
when I had no voice   Brother   I could not clear

my throat from the polluted lies and fog of the White Man

Dans l'Amerique   the bridge   then in the dawn
of my fifteenth year
was still too wide   to cross to reach you
as you stood Caesarean entropic   ready   austere
with the robe to pass on as a prophet of the *Tiers Monde*★
of your eloquence electrifying
and disturbing the air (as it still does)

She was there even then the woman I loved
but she cupped her ears   O Singer   as
seas rolled between us   in the horizon of the Poem

And it is only now (5.58 AM, a Sunday)
the words come so late having waited
so long in the wake of the odes of elegiasts obviated

2013

★*Tiers Monde*, Fr., The Third World

RÉVERIE

for Yvette Mimeux on her 71ˢᵗ birthday

> *que j'en garde ton memoire*
> ("that I keep in your memory")
> —St.-John Perse, *Chant pour un equinox*

My pen still warm as I grasp it this day
it has remained enclosed
in my pocket throughout the night
As yours is the first name I write
This day
It's as if I had never ceased
writing your name

C'est votre présence encore que m'étonné★

I am amazed
as a young goddess enters my room
veiled and bathed in yellow
under the Sign of Capricorn
her light fills the room   blonde   diaphanous
en train with my lost youth

Agon of endless hours
the painter of the Sistine Chapel up on a ladder
The "riddle of history" remains for us
unsolved   Africa's torment   The West perplexed
For these I have no ready answers
Yet I oppose "the regret of being in this world"
It is as if I had never ceased
writing your name

8ᵗʰ January, 2014

★*C'est votre présence encore que m'étonné, Fr.,* "It's your presence still that amazed me"

Note: **Yvette Mimieux**, an American film and television actress, had her breakout role in *The Time Machine* (1960). She died on January 17, 2022, about a week after her 80ᵗʰ birthday.

34

THE ROAD AHEAD... *APRÈS/*AVANT

for Richard Waara

The sunrise behind me
the moon still ahead in the sky
as I walk this morning to be awake
which is always a challenge
but then there's the fragrance
of freshly baked bread

                             At the café a woman arrives
to greet her friends "I just got out of bed!"
Myself an emergent agoraphobe again
en route like a deer taking its first steps in the forest

O sleepwalkers!
Adept organizers that lead humanity in tow
O into the abyss that is "this world"

Multitasking gurus, face-saving engineers of pogroms, social mo-
res, Remembrance Day and goal-setters—Excuse me, it's 3:18PM

                             Now a week later I've forgotten to
pay my newspaper delivery bill
The blind guy on the bus asks to "get off
at 24-Hour Fitness" "Next stop, Sir!"

It seems the more I sleep the more it is that poetry thrives
which might well be my proposal
to the Communist Party of Cyprus "debating strategy for the
    road ahead"
but I haven't posted my letter as of yet

                                        16th March, 2014

35

FOR SAMUEL "RIBITCH" MARTIN (1946-2015)

Nous nous perpetuons
("We perpetuate ourselves")
—Paul Éluard, *Capitale de la douleur*

Standing in the middle of my room   I go about
in circles this morning   half asleep
I've put my shirt on backwards again feeling overcome
by the world's problems
and being unable to reverse them

I don't know what to do with myself
except perhaps reset my shadow
and whether to view the world standing upright
or upside down as my criteria
for judging the City of God or the City of Man
embedded in the centuries of our errors
and of the perception the sea and the desert contend

In the inner landscape between my ears
my footsteps erased in the dust of Akkad
I realize O woman of my life that were I to wait for you
it would take as long as that unfolding epic
in the person of an Afro-American man sitting there
as he bides his time while white whiskers gather momentum
    (who knows how many picket lines he has manned
and maintained against the riot-controlling police?)

Ein Heldenleben   A hero's life unassuming
    El Guapo   factótum
who turns a millstone into a saxophone
    thereby insuring
the permanent revolution in days to come

24th April, 2014

36

FROM THE DUST OF BALZAC

for Richard Waara

Again the hoofbeats of Agincourt recur
galloping across my carpeted floor
As I move my dinner plate away
I cannot explain now the twitch in my eye from
which the centurion at the Crucifixion was healed
at the moment blood spilled onto his face

A hurricane rages on in my head thus
as you read this (if there is an audience out there)
F.Y.I. as the average attention-span is less than
20 minutes in America
                    I hail you
from my cave   haunted by the beatific vision of
Albert Einstein who gazes from my wall
and by the reliquary of Anne Waldman's black fishnet
stockings which once caught my sperm

Ah, Cyrenian, you've shed your shadow!
I am stabbed by my own pen during sleep
And there the River Lethe flows fluid and accessible
It carries my cry to transform myself as the Other

                              June, 2014

37

IN THE HEAT OF AUGUST

for Maya

> *Au hasard une epopée mais bien finie maintenant*
> ("Randomly an epic but well finished now")
> —Paul Éluard, *Capitale de la douleur*

The snowmen are hungry

The islands are glad   clad in their orange and yellow
                    (I hear them   as
                            they speak animatedly)

You are twelve years old

I listen   Today without sandwiches
The house wears its vibrant yellow shirt
                            of Mayakovsky

I am again an orphan of the Orient
this afternoon

My eyebrows have returned after
their nightly journey

I recognize that the glory of Africa is long gone
with the footsteps of the Queen of Sheba

The ghost of Bob Kaufman still haunts
San Francisco's North Beach

My granddaughter is dressed in her finery

O sentinels of Today

21st May—21st August, 2014

"CROSSING THE DAYS OFF THE CALENDAR"

for Timothy R. Johnson

> The minutes pass as though through sharp thorns
> —Philip Lamantia, *Erotic Poems*

As I take down from the shelf and open
pages of an old book
I discover my former wife's notes written in the margins
This morning with the hand of a usurper (Macbeth)
But there is no king to murder
Yet the spectral dagger lingers there in midair
    calling   ATTENTION   ATTENTION

Information *sur* dominion
Vous devez★
with demands of
production and conditions
of existence of the whole of humanity (Gramsci)
I again discover I have dominion
yet with nothing but seemingly illegible signposts
en route the faint-sounding horn of a car
in lieu of the unicorn's hoofsteps

I hold before me the recent letter of the woman I love
a concertina can't be made out of it   turning
one's head to the left
        For the *Entrepreneur*★★
on the oneiric
venue of transcendence

O is that whorehouse in Arles
now a sanctuary
where Van Gogh deposited his severed ear?

29th September, 2014

★ *Vous devez*, Fr., You have to
★★*Entrepreneur*, Fr., derives from the Old French meaning to undertake a task.

SPECTRE OF THE ROSE

for Dr. Elizabeth Bone, M.D.

> *C'est feu! L'ame errante se transforme en toi*
> ("It's fire! The wandering soul turns into you")
> —Author not verifiable

A telephone ringing as if spindrift "in an hour"
I find myself a castaway upon an unknown sea
where I would take refuge
beneath your white dress
in the flutter of its cotillions of lingerie

Out of a page of Byron's scrawl that's *Don Juan*
I chimney-sweep with my pen
an apogee and diadem overtaken by you
bereft of skill
O athletes of the Casamance!

(Only the melanin hidden in my skin remains)

An anatomy class in progress   I, *Nuncio*
and *Nuncle* of the displayed skeleton

"Observer"   Builder of cities and their destroyer

Cower now as a cowled monk I take shelter
in my bower as my gaze drifts toward an empty pack
of "Doral Lights" thrust in the wastebasket by a passerby

     ROOM NO. 5
From there I plot the hoofbeats of Man
across the undulating expanse of the GEONOM
Its DNA patterns absolve and dissolve
As you confide to me if only momentarily a girlhood
recaptured "amidst blossoming hills in Amherst"

1994—2014

40

COSMOGONY REALIZED

for Will Alexander

Conduisent à l'amour marque sur chaque porte
("Leading to love marked on every door")
—Robert Desnos, *Trois Étoiles*

I need not travel far
from this place here where I sit and am still
to find the refuge
with the Silence
          As the nave
of the sanctuary of rock-hewn Aksum
There in my presence
All things come to birth

As Kekrops founded Athens its Primal Poet
to tell all
beyond the tomfoolery of man
The splendour of a woman's lithe leg and in her voice

We come to the Number 8 portal to infinity
a road map for future generations
never realized before
in my youth's mathematical "mental block"

Ah, theorems of Pythagoras that left me wanting
And then finding myself in the wake of the artist's realm
standing before Pollock's *Summertime: Number 9A* as it
transmitted to my mind its Terra Incognita

For perpetual discovery in search
of the Seeress in the Woman I love   She who is
l'absente
      but ever *present* in this omphalic module

17th—18th June, 2015

41

RÊVE À DEUX

for Richard Waara

There is a recurring joust between good and evil
in the world
It is here that I find myself fallen
knight in the midst of the clamour
who rises again somehow
to rejoin the fray

I realize it is the dream I am in that goes on

Keeping me hanging there
clinging onto the beard of Simeon Stylites
who looks down at me in the desert
laughing at me dangling there
still trying to drain the seawater from my ears

I recognize distance
measured by
the space that separates me from the woman I love

The Hitchhiker's Guide to the Galaxy
postulates the number 42
as the answer to the Ultimate Question

As for myself I walk on terra firma
to lift the day and "fill it" with my pen

I realize this must be the signal
to awaken and be reconstituted to my real self
Although I refuse to play chess as a challenger
to Mendel's dominant and recessive genes
on the gridiron of Life

11th November 2015

42

SERENATA NOTTURNA

for Signora Carla Chigi-Nalon (in Rome, Italy)

sei ritornata limpida ai baloni
("you returned limpid to the balconies")
—Salvatore Quasimodo, *Elégia*

Again as I sit here it nears

Like Pushkin at work by candlelight at verses
   for *Eugène Onégin*
I look out on the world
O stones of Rome   blood imprinted therein
of early martyrs unseen
by the flock of tourists strolling past the Pantheon
I dip my pen in it with the daylight

Facing the Abyss
and the summit
of human consciousness
          Here where her portrait like an
       Egyptian princess of the XIX Dynasty
stares out at me

As I wrestle down the griffin's wings

There before me lie all the dreams
of the great Liberators
        Bolivar / Lumumba
   Kwame Nkrumah / Allende / Che Guevara

As I find myself idling in my kitchen

I hear that song of Groucho Marx play once again
in my head: "Hello, I must be going!"
    Someone who saw
Or can give a firsthand account
of something that "happened"

43

                              Here the gaping
space that clamours
on the canvas for the painter Diego Rivera to complete

As the Poem's ambuscade awaits
where I find myself devoid of words

As misdeeds and foibles of our species increase

I, an agoraphobe, sequestered
in the solitude of my room

In the Silence presented by the East aflame
with the sunrise a prize

Which I hold
as a delicate flower

                                        December, 2015

44

LE BILLET DOUX

for Bill Berkson

> *feux tessous perdus en un désert de peurs et de citernes*
> ("fires shards lost in a desert of fears and cisterns")
> —Aimé Césaire, *Ferraments*

It's Saturday again
At the moment I am thinking of
Fragonard's *Le Billet Doux* then draw a blank

Look what the Wright Bros. have done for us!
"Surgical bombings" over Tikrit
My paranoia needs Venetian-blinds and bodies
moving between the trees and the sun

The synapses aren't connecting properly   However
I keep on thinking   I might
rediscover Archimedes' principle
but I have no crown to float in the bathtub

Across the way the caravan of emigrés continues on
            moving from this locale to
I-know-not-where

Pharoah's snake becomes fossil fuel (the price
of oil on the stock market) "Love ever exciting and new"
It is Woman who is the true Kaaba waiting
            to be kissed by the pilgrim

23rd February, 2016

INCANTATION

for Will Alexander

*My imagination is my Monastery and
I am its Monk* —John Keats, *Letters*

Endlessly feeling this time is ripe
to try new things
But still in search of a hope
in the external world (though I have always
had one in the internal)
Tchaikovsky's triumph over fate
whose distance or remoteness
is reckoned miles from Los Angeles

My coffee cup sits lonely on the bench
as Mevia's letter still salutes me
"Buon Santo Natale"★ at my bedside
while "boomer women" lead the wave
of aging workers making furniture tip-proof

I wait for the simurgh bird
to provide transportation to new vistas
now that Moscow's domes and testimonies
are left behind in my Yonnondio'ing★★

Wait in stillness for the sounding
the comings and goings of footsteps that bypass
the Sunday newspaper left at their door-sill
as a gratuity which hearkens back
to the upbraiding of Chorazin

Yet the prescient Arcane 17 star
still manifests its ascendant for you

9th April, 2016

★*"Buon Santo Natale,"* *It.,* Merry Christmas
★★ "Yonnondio" ('ing) Title of a poem from Walt Whitman's *Leaves of Grass.*
Whitman said this word for the Iroquois means "lament."

46

I WOULD SUMMON BEAUTY FOR YOU

for Mm. Sandra Morineau

> *D'avoir d'être vivants nous continuons*
> ("To stay alive we must continue on")
> —Paul Éluard, *Blason dédoré de mes rêves*

I would summon beauty for you
in these pages   But it seems
to elude me   each time
in a broken landscape   a deserted dwelling

Hunger... in a land gleaming rich harvests

Homeless...wandering cadres   seeking refuge in doorstops

Dawn breaking over
war-torn ruins between the Tigris and the Euphrates

A flea appears
out-of-nowhere   then hops from one place to another

Onto a pile of unpaid bills and papers
in lieu of love letters   The words of a poem
appearing in a dream and then vanishing upon waking

I would summon beauty for you
hanging by a thread
from my tattered shirtsleeve

In the leaves scattered by the wind
and then tossed onto my threshold

In the vision of a Seer
which reaches beyond the boundaries of space and time

7th April, 2017

47

ON THE NIGHT OF THE MARCH OF EVIL

for Alexis and Sofia Rosinsky

> *Et nous recondruirons aux portes de la Ville*
> ("And we shall usher out at the gates of the City")
> —St.-John Perse, ***Pluies***

On the night of the March of Evil
Death sounded the drums amid the howls
and imprecations
and lit the tiki-torches of the marchers
While Life waited for those who resisted
with the same cry once cried out from the barricades—
¡NO PASARÀN!

On the night of the March of Evil
was witnessed beneath the lintels
History repeating itself in the *ordure* of
a bevy of grave-robbers and a host of ghosts
exulting the fiendish carnage of Auschwitz

On the day after the March of Evil
the defenders on the side of Life prevailed
though not unscathed
a young woman* would not see daylight again
but Charlottesville will henceforth be emblazoned
    with—Madrid   Lexington   Harper's Ferry
the Warsaw Ghetto   Sharpeville   Pettus Bridge/Selma

On the day after the March of Evil
the defenders of Life formed their human phalanx
and would once again triumph
against the purveyors of Death

11th—12th August, 2017

*Ms. Heather Danielle Heyer (May 29,1985-August 12, 2017)

48

TO YÉGHISHÉ CHARENTS, THE MAYAKOVSKY
  OF ARMENIA

De nouveau tu me soulèves, souvenir
("Again you lift me up, memory")
—L.S. Senghor, *Élégies majeures*

O trampled land! O trampled soul!
Where in your cell
all of history yet roams and awaits the day
of resurrection   A withered hand writes
inscribing in blood on the wall—
l'Armenie, l'Armenie vivant!

Soundless
the perpetual wound in my breast

Names of forebears I will never know
Entombed on the road to the Syrian desert
The dogwood flower glows day and night
tended lovingly by an unseen woman's hand
which in turn
soothes the sweat from your brow

—Whose child is *Anahid*
culled from the black mirror of memory

People speak of words
but don't know that they are born in blood
A man can die for speaking them!
A woman's life turned around in a second!

O of words! Bound for a lifetime
of servitude or for the garden of Serendip!

Where in your cell, my brother
all of history yet roams
through the dark night of the soul that awaits the day

14ᵗʰ October, 2017

49

Marie Wilson: *Eagle Spirit*, India ink, 1976–77

MIGRATION OF IMMORTALITY

for Marie Wilson-Valaoritis (1922-2017)

> *...de faire revivre les êtres qui me manquent*
> ("...to bring back to life the persons I miss")
> —André Breton, *"Rideau rideau"*

In the domain of the undiscovered
estuary of the Uncertainty Principle
Marie's secret remains

Yet unfolding
as the Ziziphus lotus cannot be duplicated

Between dream and waking in this our mesmeric world
the spaces that come between
I cannot account for

It is the clouds who are the guardians which remain
prescient upholders of the Goddess myth

As do these lines capture in perpetuity
the *viola d'amore* of her benignity
and that of the legendary queen of Armenia

Once more I find myself in the presence of
the grand catalogue of hybrid roses
transplanted from the Near East
to Malmaison
bereft of its regal gardener

In the midst of this barren land
of my own bewilderment

At the succession of *bienvenues* and *adieus*

As dawn descants on the African Savannah

With the precision of an icon-painter's brush
the architecture of snowflakes assume
each their own assigned singular form

                          "Having reached
the station of unity"

                   Beyond Sun and Moon
Marie holds
concourse
        with the Seeress Diotima

On the gradual of assents to Love

In the autotelic realm of the Eidolon

                        22nd October, 2017

ON THE ONGOING FEMICIDES IN MEXICO

for María Elena Salinas & Gerónimo Sarmiento Cruz

Countless rows of murdered women to date now lie silent
underground   Silent with the flowers
waiting for each Spring   Silent
with the vigilant stars overhead
which guard the plain below   Silent now
with music at their *quinceañeras**
Silent with their white dresses in the photographs
as a memento for an occasion...

Silent as the Jacaranda
cast amongst dismembered hearts   turned to dust
cut out by Aztec priests before the *Conquesta*
in exchange to the gods for a rich harvest
young bodies of girls and boys cast down the temple stairs
the beauty of their limbs as refuse into the ground

Silent as the Jacaranda
which no longer can embrace friend or lover
or no longer can flatter feet in elegant shoes
amongst the shell cases of the fatal bullets that
cut down the revolutionary Emiliano Zapata

Silent as the ages
as the passing days
amidst the archaeologist's finds of buried weapons
and armour of the conquistadors...
Silent as the "broken spears" of the jaguar warriors...
Silent as the Jacaranda

2020

quinceañeras, in Latin America a celebration of a girl's fifteenth birthday and her
transition from childhood to adulthood.

LOUISE BROOKS' LEGS

for C. Brooke Rothwell

Louise Brooks' legs
shine over Hollywood like a new moon
I embraced them before my birth
signed my name upon them
in invisible semen ink

Their ship's captain throughout
seas of skulduggery in the offing
each time she exhibited them for
onlookers in the storm of entropy
as she obliterated all meaning to
the human endeavor
and then restored it to herself

The book of Hollywood catches fire
with all except her photos
Louise Brooks' whiteness as against
my darkness

What will oracular drummers of
the Siné-Saloum have to say?

Just that we bow
and pay our homage as mortals
We whom are ever exiled
from the realm of the gods

2nd February, 2021

54

THE DARKNESS HAS NOT PREVAILED

for my Nurse, Chana'ah, R.N.

> *Femme, pose sur mon front tes mains balsamiques*
> ("Woman, lay your hands of balsam on my forehead")
> —L.S. Senghor, *Chants d'ombre*

The darkness has not prevailed
to swallow you up into nothingness

As the maelstrom of demonic madmen swept over
your country of the horsemen of the Khmers
it took so many lives into the abyss

Yet you survived   Somehow   rose up
from a vanquished land   bearing in yourself
its innate beauty and elegance

You opened the door to my being
            as caregiver to my life / the trauma
which clenched unremittingly   and ground
my teeth at night
The poet's body
whose functions at times
interfere with poetry

From centuries of exilement   the soul's
infinitude   in flight
fathomless   the mystery you eluded
the monsters and their "killing fields"

The darkness has not prevailed

            in ourselves

        both *inermé*★

as emigrés to this land

Where justice cries out yet still
for redress
as I myself mouth George Floyd's
last words to America "I can't breathe!"

As our paths intersect
in the moment
of this *Altérnité**/systole and diastole*
long-awaited

You bring *balm in Gilead****
to anoint my brow and soothe

wounded souls
Patient and Nurse

February, 2021

MEMORIAL DAY

In Memoriam Ted Berrigan (1934-1983)

THERE'S NOTHING GOING ON TODAY INSIDE THE STATUE OF LIBERTY'S HEAD

Nothing
but useless trash on TV
Can you imagine someone
saying this to Samuel Taylor Coleridge circa 1825?
(I didn't think so.)

Nothing to do but
learn to write letters again
Thanks to the Sumerian's gift of cuneiform
and Birthday Wishes
from Ace Hardware

So happens another Memorial Day
that folds into history
The woman I once loved has long ago disappeared
She left me with only her footprint
and moved to Indianapolis
where race cars wait all year in their stalls
to zoom zoom zoom their engines again

From afar
an African Griot looks on at the spectacle
and says "What the hell's all this good for anyway?"
(No one living can respond.)

31st May, 2021

57

VAN GOGH LEFT HIS SEVERED BLOODY EAR AS VESTIGE

for Collin Schuster

> *Les temps aussi de regler leur compite a quelques*
> *fantasme et a quelques fantomes*
> ("The times also settle their account with a few
> fantasies and a few ghosts")—Aimé Césaire,
> *Moi, laminaire*

Van Gogh left his severed bloody ear as vestige

What then would you have me leave
O my elusive fey?

This wanderer's heart
which never seems to be satisfied
and betrays my ardour with my enemies?

You will ask "What enemies?"

They are the stray hours and minutes of the day
and the day's thoughts I cannot capture or subdue
that impish play of hide-and-go-seek with myself
which thwarts my life's trajectory

This pen in hand which I always seem to lose
as it slips from my fingers while jotting down
that which comes in the interim of day or night

This hand so long a faithful
servant of my lifelong endeavors
which upon command proves itself
a worthy witness to my own identity
that often escapes me during the day's ennui

Or these eyes with their weakened vision
which often lose their focus
as if in a foreign terrain

What am I then?
To sever these from myself and send
them on their way

Or better yet
what of this book which is in itself
part and parcel of my lifeblood?

What of these of its pages that verge with
the names of those I have loved?

Will they urge on—or garner—or enliven
Or be tossed in the fire as tares?

June, 2021

AUTOMATIQUE/07.12.2021

for Collin Schuster

The thought of eating today
makes me feel ill   I want to eat books instead
digest them and then become all-encompassing
in knowledge like the great Sphinx

Flora lives somewhere in the dolomites
Fauna is right here beneath my feet
the earth's surface where men forage
for food that eventually turn to feces
which then becomes rock again
specimens perhaps which Emily Sanagorski
will explore in the Carlsbad Caverns
where its caves wail and moan

I go hungry like the anchorites of old
to gain this one line each day out of the blue
I begin in lieu of Diogenes' lantern
whose light searched for "one honest man"
although I have forgone the search long ago

O wild and loose my soul!
We trod on in this Fool's Paradise here
as Earth Air Fire and Water provide
the alchemist his wares
Flora and fauna where we begin and end

SCHEMATA

for Chelsea, my Caregiver

"What convulses" is
this: that reality as we know it by
is but a sham of the senses' drollery
spurious as I
who step outside
my shadow
to perpetuate

The unsayable beyond space and time

And thus forget
quotidian exigencies pending appointments
and dates
socks cannot speak nor hold courts

Nor the jack-o'-lanterns that are risible in the span
of months as I note
to say "good morning" to you as
you enter through a *point d'Alençon* curtain

"Pregnancy 101" clicks on your computer screen
to my world each day's
schedule of "things to do" which overcome
and then return
to our respective distances at day's end

Duties and errands
assigned in the interim
of your venue the trees keep in themselves
trove in retrospect
The *gratis*
that is bestowed and held

13th July, 2021

AUTOMATIQUE *AU-DELÀ*

for Thom Burns

As China dissolves to AstroTurf and foolscap...

There is yet another stair for me to ascend
to reach that infinite prospect
where I will again encounter Ibn al-Arabi
To retrieve my own name
from the domain of the Gods

Lest still here with this mayhem of players
in their scrambled formations
As I rub the lustrous hole in my head
to discharge the fount of wisdom
latent in the interior of my medulla oblongata
And yet here the realm of dreams lies unclaimed
where the efficacy of economics and politics
still holds sway (here with all due reference to
    Baran & Sweezy's exegesis)

To prophecy within the bounds of
"real world numbers" as defense against
the capitalist despoilers of the world
Yet my *bienvenue** goes out to all those
bound for their own endeavor
to individually mount
the upward path of *au-delà***

2021

*bienvenue, Fr., welcome & **au-delà, Fr., beyond

Note: *Monopoly Capital: An Essay on the American Economic and Social Order*
(1966) by Marxist economists Paul Baran and Paul Sweezy has been used since it first
appeared as a textbook on economics in American universities and colleges.

T^{ABLE} O^F P^{OEMS}

Le labyrinthe
qui remonte la valleuse à toute allure
et brûle toutes les
mosquées »   XX19 — S.T.

The labyrinth
   "which traces back up the valley at full speed
and burns all the
       mosques"

                        XX19—S.T.

Ainsi,
« tulipe, il se trouve que quelqu'un
vous a vu dans mon bureau »
comme ceci la poésie es défectible
                         — 10. ii. 2021
                              J. T.

In this way,
"tulip, someone happening
to see you in my office"
like this poetry is defeasible
                    —10. ii. 2021
                         S.T.

CPSIA information can be obtained
at www.ICGtesting.com
Printed in the USA
LVHW021500310323
743154LV00028B/832

9 781411 688742